GRADE 1

MATH Trailblazers®

A BALANCED MATHEMATICS PROGRAM INTEGRATING SCIENCE AND LANGUAGE ARTS

Student Guide

Book 2

THIRD EDITION

KENDALL/HUNT PUBLISHING COMPANY
4050 Westmark Drive   Dubuque, Iowa 52002

A TIMS® Curriculum
University of Illinois at Chicago

MATH TRAILBLAZERS®

Dedication

This book is dedicated to
the children and teachers who
let us see the magic in their classrooms
and to our families who wholeheartedly
supported us while we searched for
ways to make it happen.

The TIMS Project

  The University of Illinois at Chicago

The original edition was based on work supported by the National Science Foundation under grant No. MDR 9050226 and the University of Illinois at Chicago. Any opinions, findings, and conclusions or recommendations expressed in this publication are those of the authors and do not necessarily reflect the views of the granting agencies.

Acknowledgments

Teaching Integrated Mathematics and Science (TIMS) Project Directors
Philip Wagreich, Principal Investigator
Joan L. Bieler
Howard Goldberg (emeritus)
Catherine Randall Kelso

Principal Investigators

First Edition	Philip Wagreich
	Howard Goldberg

Directors

Third Edition	Joan L. Bieler
Second Edition	Catherine Randall Kelso

Senior Curriculum Developers

First Edition	Janet Simpson Beissinger	Carol Inzerillo
	Joan L. Bieler	Andy Isaacs
	Astrida Cirulis	Catherine Randall Kelso
	Marty Gartzman	Leona Peters
	Howard Goldberg	Philip Wagreich

Curriculum Developers

Third Edition	Janet Simpson Beissinger	Philip Wagreich
Second Edition	Lindy M. Chambers-Boucher	Jennifer Mundt Leimberer
	Elizabeth Colligan	Georganne E. Marsh
	Marty Gartzman	Leona Peters
	Carol Inzerillo	Philip Wagreich
	Catherine Randall Kelso	
First Edition	Janice C. Banasiak	Jenny Knight
	Lynne Beauprez	Sandy Niemiera
	Andy Carter	Janice Ozima
	Lindy M. Chambers-Boucher	Polly Tangora
	Kathryn Chval	Paul Trafton
	Diane Czerwinski	

Illustrator

	Kris Dresen

Editorial and Production Staff

Third Edition	Kathleen R. Anderson	Christina Clemons
	Lindy M. Chambers-Boucher	
Second Edition	Kathleen R. Anderson	Georganne E. Marsh
	Ai-Ai C. Cojuangco	Cosmina Menghes
	Andrada Costoiu	Anne Roby
	Erika Larson	
First Edition	Glenda L. Genio-Terrado	Sarah Nelson
	Mini Joseph	Biruté Petrauskas
	Lynelle Morgenthaler	

Acknowledgments

TIMS Professional Developers

Barbara Crum	Cheryl Kneubuhler
Catherine Ditto	Lisa Mackey
Pamela Guyton	Linda Miceli

TIMS Director of Media Services

Henrique Cirne-Lima

TIMS Research Staff

Stacy Brown	Catherine Ditto
Reality Canty	Catherine Randall Kelso

TIMS Administrative Staff

Eve Ali Boles	Enrique Puente
Kathleen R. Anderson	Alice VanSlyke
Nida Khan	

Research Consultant

First Edition   Andy Isaacs

Mathematics Education Consultant

First Edition   Paul Trafton

National Advisory Committee

First Edition

Carl Berger	Mary Lindquist
Tom Berger	Eugene Maier
Hugh Burkhardt	Lourdes Monteagudo
Donald Chambers	Elizabeth Phillips
Naomi Fisher	Thomas Post
Glenda Lappan	

TIMS Project Staff

Table of Contents

Additional student pages may be found in the *Adventure Book*
or the *Unit Resource Guide*.

Table of Contents

Additional student pages may be found in the *Adventure Book* or the *Unit Resource Guide*.

Dear Parents,

Math Trailblazers® is based on the ideas that mathematics is best learned through solving many different kinds of problems and that all children deserve a challenging mathematics curriculum. The program provides a careful balance of concepts and skills. Traditional arithmetic skills and procedures are covered through their repeated use in problems and through distributed practice. *Math Trailblazers,* however, offers much more. Students using this program will become proficient problem solvers, will know when and how to apply the mathematics they have

learned, and will be able to clearly communicate their mathematical knowledge. Computation, measurement, geometry, data collection and analysis, estimation, graphing, patterns and relationships, mental arithmetic, and simple algebraic ideas are all an integral part of the curriculum. They will see connections between the mathematics learned in school and the mathematics used in everyday life. And, they will enjoy and value the work they do in mathematics.

The *Student Guide* is only one component of *Math Trailblazers*. Additional material and lessons are contained in the *Adventure Book* and in the teacher's *Unit Resource Guides.* If you have questions about the program, we encourage you to speak with your child's teacher.

This curriculum was built around national recommendations for improving mathematics instruction in American schools and the research that supported those recommendations. The first edition was extensively tested with thousands of children in dozens of classrooms over five years of development. In preparing the second and third editions, we have benefited from the comments and suggestions of hundreds of teachers and children who have used the curriculum. *Math Trailblazers* reflects our view of a complete and well-balanced mathematics program that will prepare children for the 21st century—a world in which mathematical skills will be important in most occupations and mathematical reasoning will be essential for acting as an informed citizen in a democratic society. We hope that you enjoy this exciting approach to learning mathematics and that you watch your child's mathematical abilities grow throughout the year.

Philip Wagreich

Philip Wagreich
Professor, Department of Mathematics, Statistics, and Computer Science
Director, Institute for Mathematics and Science Education
Teaching Integrated Mathematics and Science (TIMS) Project
University of Illinois at Chicago

Unit 11

Looking at 100

	Student Guide	Adventure Book	Unit Resource Guide*
Lesson 1			
100 Links	●		
Lesson 2			
Pennies and Dimes	●		
Lesson 3			
Dimes, Nickels, and Quarters	●		
Lesson 4			
Arrow Dynamics	●		
Lesson 5			
How Long Is 100?	●		
Lesson 6			
Weather 2: Winter Skies	●		●
Lesson 7			
It's Sunny in Arizona	●	●	
Lesson 8			
Maria's Marble Mart	●		

*Unit Resource Guide pages are from the teacher materials.

100-Link Chain

Two Parts

Break your chain into two parts. Count the number of links in each part. Then, write a number sentence.

_____ + _____ = _____

Three Parts

Break your chain into three parts. Count the number of links in each part. Then, write a number sentence.

_____ + _____ + _____ = _____

Find three more ways to break the chain into three parts. Write a number sentence for each.

_____ + _____ + _____ = _____

_____ + _____ + _____ = _____

_____ + _____ + _____ = _____

Pennies

You have 10 pennies to put into two piles. Do this in many ways. Write a number sentence for each. Then, put the 10 pennies into 3 piles. Write a number sentence.

Pennies
_____ + _____ = 10
_____ + _____ = 10
_____ + _____ = 10
10 = _____ + _____
10 = _____ + _____
10 – _____ = _____
10 – _____ = _____
10 – _____ = _____
_____ + _____ + _____ = 10

Dimes

Arrange 10 dimes into two piles. Then, find other ways to arrange the 10 dimes. Write an addition number sentence for each. Write subtraction number sentences, too.

Dimes
_____ + _____ = 100
_____ + _____ = 100
_____ + _____ = 100
100 = _____ + _____
100 = _____ + _____
100 − _____ = _____
100 − _____ = _____
100 − _____ = _____
100 − _____ = _____
100 − _____ = _____

Name _____ Date _____

Three Piles

Divide your group of dimes into three piles. How many different ways can you think of?

_____ + _____ + _____ = 100

_____ + _____ + _____ = 100

_____ + _____ + _____ = 100

_____ + _____ + _____ = 100

_____ + _____ + _____ = 100

_____ + _____ + _____ = 100

_____ + _____ + _____ = 100

_____ + _____ + _____ = 100

Name _____   Date _____

Starting with 100

Homework

Dear Family Member:

Your child divided 10 dimes into two piles and wrote number sentences to describe the partitions. A number sentence for 8 dimes and 2 dimes is 80 + 20 = 100 cents.

Help your child fill in the missing numbers and write subtraction sentences for the problems that follow. To solve 60 + _____ = 100, for example, your child might place a real dime or a piece of cereal on 6 of the dimes in the picture. Then, he or she can skip count by tens to find the value of the 4 uncovered dimes. Your child may also want to cut out the dimes at the bottom of the page. Thank you for your cooperation.

Find the missing numbers. Write two subtraction sentences for each addition sentence. Use the dimes to help you.

90 + __10__ = 100	60 + _____ = 100
100 – 90 = __10__	100 – 60 = _____
100 – __10__ = 90	

_____ + 70 = 100

80 + _____ = 100

Find the missing numbers.

50 + _____ = 100

100 − 50 = _____

Name _____ Date _____

Twins' Day at the County Fair

Draw different ways the twins can make $1.00. Then, record the amount of money from each twin.

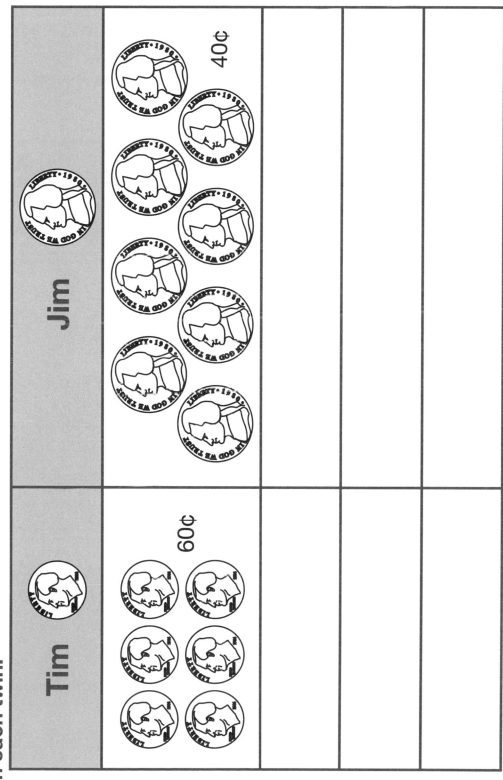

Tim	Jim
60¢	40¢

Shuttle Bus #100

Shuttle bus #100 carries exactly 100 people each trip. It stops at three different parking lots. The people are picked up in groups of ten. The bus driver records the number of people picked up at each stop. Fill in the missing numbers on his chart. You can use beans on the number strip to help you.

10	10	10	10	10	10	10	10	10	10

Parking Lot 1		**Parking Lot 2**		**Parking Lot 3**	
20	+	50	+	_____	= 100
40	+	40	+	_____	= 100
10	+	60	+	_____	= 100
_____	+	20	+	60	= 100
60	+	_____	+	40	= 100
30	+	_____	+	40	= 100
50	+	40	+	_____	= 100
80	+	10	+	_____	= 100

Dimes, Nickels, and Quarters

Shuttle Bus #50

Homework

Shuttle bus #50 carries exactly 50 people each trip. The bus stops at three different parking lots. The people are picked up in groups of five. Help the driver fill in the missing numbers on his chart. You can use beans on the number strip to help you.

5	5	5	5	5	5	5	5	5	5

Parking Lot 1		Parking Lot 2		Parking Lot 3	
25	+	5	+	_____	= 50
10	+	30	+	_____	= 50
15	+	_____	+	20	= 50
5	+	_____	+	35	= 50
_____	+	20	+	10	= 50
25	+	_____	+	20	= 50
40	+	_____	+	5	= 50
25	+	15	+	_____	= 50

Arrow Dynamics Game Board

Players

This is a game for two or more players.

Materials

- *100 Chart*
- clear spinner (or paper clip and pencil)
- game markers

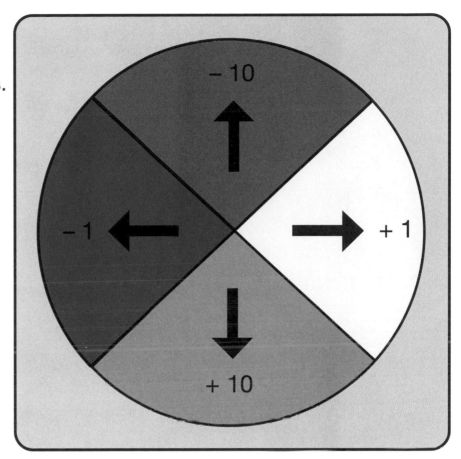

Rules

1. Each player places a marker on the number 45 on the *100 Chart*. Use the rules below and take turns.

2. Spin. Move your marker one space in the direction shown.

3. Say a number sentence that describes your move. Then, write it on your record sheet. Example: Start at 45. Move up one space. $45 - 10 = 35$.

4. The player who reaches the largest number after 7 spins wins.

100 Chart

1	2	3	4	5	6	7	8	9	10
11	12	13	14	15	16	17	18	19	20
21	22	23	24	25	26	27	28	29	30
31	32	33	34	35	36	37	38	39	40
41	42	43	44	45	46	47	48	49	50
51	52	53	54	55	56	57	58	59	60
61	62	63	64	65	66	67	68	69	70
71	72	73	74	75	76	77	78	79	80
81	82	83	84	85	86	87	88	89	90
91	92	93	94	95	96	97	98	99	100

Arrow Dynamics Record Sheet 1

Write a number sentence to describe each move.

Player 1	Player 2

Arrow Dynamics Record Sheet 2

Write a number sentence to describe each move.

Player 1	Player 2

Name _____ Date _____

Who Is Winning?

Read the directions for playing *Arrow Dynamics*. Find the answers to the moves three players made during a game. Use your *100 Chart*.

Player 1 Starts on 45 and moves:

Lands on _____

Player 2 Starts on 45 and moves:

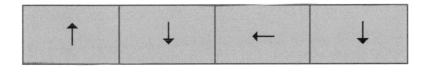

Lands on _____

Player 3 Starts on 45 and moves:

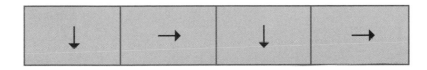

Lands on _____

The goal for the game is to have the largest number.

Which player is winning? _____

Follow the Arrows

Here are some moves in an *Arrow Dynamics* game. Write a number sentence to describe each move. Use your *100 Chart*.

1. Start on 45. Move . Land on _____

   Number Sentence: _____

2. Start on 55. Move . Land on _____

   Number Sentence: _____

3. Start on 58. Move . Land on _____

   Number Sentence: _____

4. Start on 92. Move 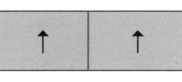. Land on _____

   Number Sentence: _____

5. Start on 12. Move 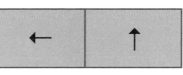. Land on _____

   Number Sentence: _____

100 Seconds

Draw one X in each box. How many Xs do you think you can draw in 100 seconds? Try it for 10 seconds and then make a prediction.

How many Xs did you draw in 10 seconds?

_____

How many Xs do you think you could draw in 100 seconds?

_____

Try it. How many Xs did you draw in 100 seconds?

_____

Look at your prediction. Were you close? Why or why not?

_____

_____

_____

_____

Name _____   Date _____

Weather 2 Calendar

Time of Day:

Month: _____   Year: _____

Sunday	Monday	Tuesday	Wednesday	Thursday	Friday	Saturday

Name _____ Date _____

Weather 2 Picture

Draw a picture of your experiment.

Weather 2 Data Table

Record your data in the table below.

Weather 2

T Type of _____	*N* Number of _____	
	Tallies	Total

Name _____ Date _____

Weather 2 Graph

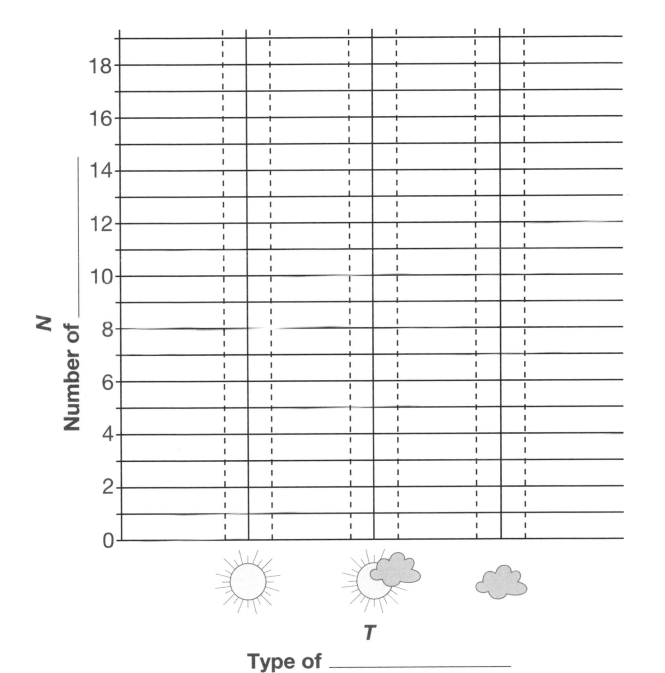

Thinking about Winter Skies

1. Which type of sky did you see *most* often?

    _____

2. Which type of sky did you see *least* often?

    _____

3. How many sunny *and* partly sunny skies were there in all?

    _____

4. Were there more cloudy skies or more sunny skies?

    _____

5. How many days are there in half of this winter month?

    _____

6. **A.** Was any type of sky seen on more than half the days

    in the month? _____

    B. Which type of sky was it? _____

Name _____ Date _____

Comparing Fall and Winter Skies

Record your data for each month's weather in the data table.

T Type of Sky _____	*N* Number of Days	
	_____ month	_____ month
☀		
⛅		
☁		

1. **A.** Which month had more sunny days?

   B. How many more? _____

   C. Is this a big difference or a small difference?

   _____

2. **A.** Which month had more partly sunny days?

_____

   B. How many more? _____

   C. Is this a big difference or a small difference?

_____

3. **A.** Which month had more cloudy days? _____

   B. How many more? _____

   C. Is this a big difference or a small difference?

_____

4. When would you expect more cloudy days—an autumn month or a winter month?

_____

How can you use the data to answer this question?

_____

_____

_____

Weather 2: Winter Skies

Name _____ Date _____

Weather Data

September's Weather

T Type of Day	N Number of Days
☀	16
⛅	5
☁	9

October's Weather

T Type of Day	N Number of Days
☀	13
⛅	14
☁	4

November's Weather

T Type of Day	N Number of Days
☀	7
⛅	8
☁	15

December's Weather

T Type of Day	N Number of Days
☀	3
⛅	11
☁	17

Weather Problems

Michael and Bianca are doing a science project. They compared the data they collected for four months. They recorded their data on the *Weather Data* Activity Page. Use this data to answer these questions.

1. How many sunny days did they record for December and November? _____

   Write a number sentence to show how you found the answer.

   _____

2. How many more cloudy days were there in September than

   in October? _____

   Write a number sentence to show how you found the answer.

   _____

3. How many days were cloudy in September and October?

   _____

   Write a number sentence to show how you found the answer.

   _____

4. They found there were 39 sunny days in the four months.

Is their total correct? _____

How did you decide?

_____

_____

_____

What is another way to find the total number of sunny days?

_____

_____

_____

_____

Think of other problems you can ask about these data tables. Write the problems in your journal.

Winter Weather

Which of the items listed below might be important in predicting the weather? Circle the best answer.

A. your grade

B. where you live

C. the number of pets you have

D. the time of year

Below are two graphs. One shows data collected in Tucson, Arizona. The other shows data collected in Chicago, Illinois. Write the story of each graph.

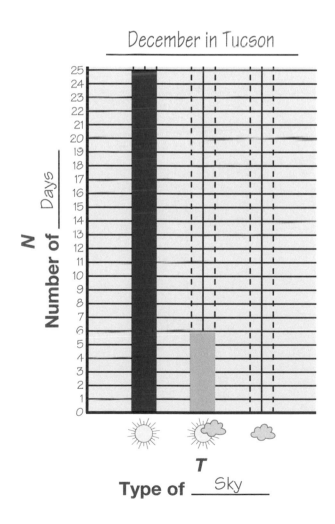

December in Tucson

_N_ Number of __Days__

_T_ Type of __Sky__

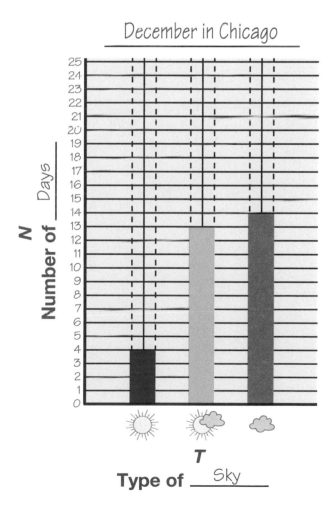

December in Chicago

_N_ Number of __Days__

_T_ Type of __Sky__

Name ——————

Date ——————

U.S.A. Map

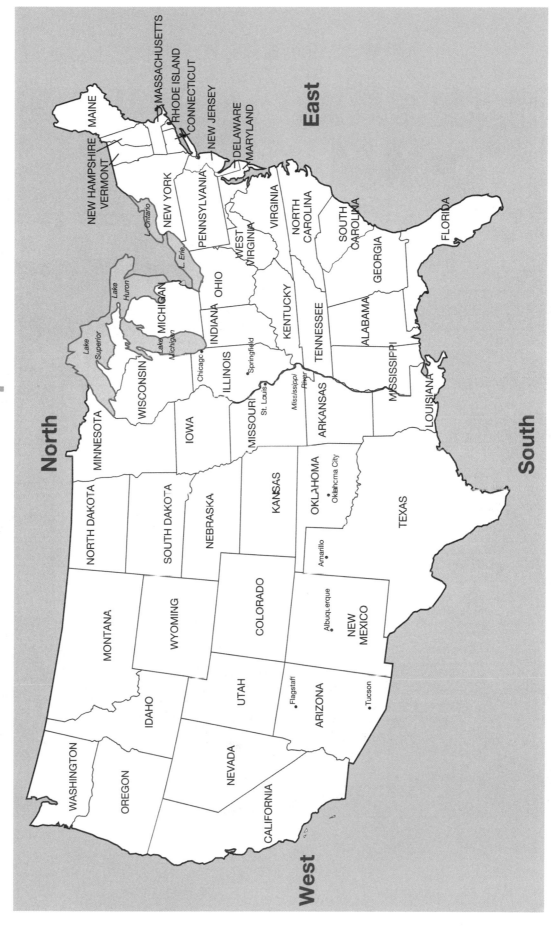

West

North

East

South

It's Sunny in Arizona

Copyright © Kendall/Hunt Publishing Company

SG • Grade 1 • Unit 11 • Lesson 7

Maria's Marble Mart

Marble Orders

Help Maria fill marble orders. Show how many of each container to use.

This order is for _____ marbles.

_____ _____ _____
tallies   tallies   tallies

_____
number sentence

This order is for _____ marbles.

_____ _____ _____
tallies   tallies   tallies

_____
number sentence

This order is for _____ marbles.

_____ _____ _____
tallies   tallies   tallies

_____
number sentence

This order is for _____ marbles.

_____ _____ _____
tallies   tallies   tallies

_____
number sentence

Cubes and Volume

	Student Guide	Adventure Book	Unit Resource Guide*
Lesson 1			
Skylines	●		
Lesson 2			
Cubic Classroom	●		
Lesson 3			
TIMS Towers	●		
Lesson 4			
A World of Cubic Animals	●	●	

*Unit Resource Guide pages are from the teacher materials.

My 8-Cube Building

1. The **area** of the floor plan in square units is _____.

2. The **volume** in cubic units is _____.

3. The **height** in number of floors is _____.

Cube Models

1. Select an object. Then, draw a picture of it.

2. Make a **life-size** cube model of the object.

3. Count the cubes to find the volume of the model. The

   volume of my cube model is _____.

4. Is the volume of the cube model **the same as**, **less than**, or **greater than** the volume of the real object? The **volume** of

   my cube model is _____ that of the real object.

Find and Model Objects

Homework

Dear Family Member:

Your child is learning to estimate volumes of objects by modeling them with connecting cubes. Help your child select an object from home to model with cubes. Please send that object to school with your child.

Thank you for your help.

Find objects in your home that you can model with connecting cubes. The objects should be about the same size as those we modeled in class. Bring an object to school to model with the cubes.

Juice Can

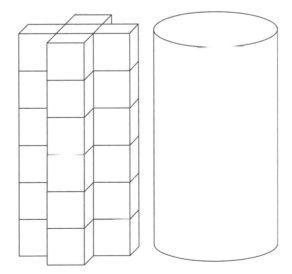

volume of cube model = 30 unit cubes

TIMS Towers 1

Use cubes to make buildings just like these. Think of different ways to find the volume of each building. Record the volume on the *TIMS Towers Data Table*.

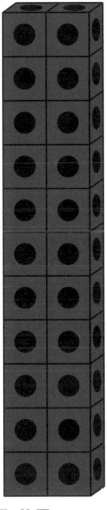

Tall Tower

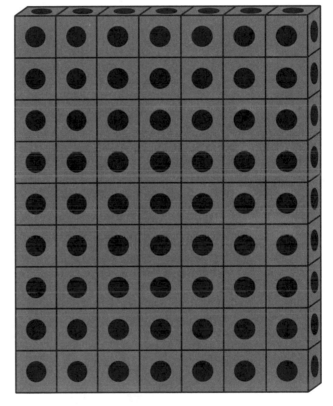

Sky-High Tower

TIMS Towers 2

Build these towers. Think of different ways to find the volume of each. Record the volume on the *TIMS Towers Data Table.*

Triple Double Tower

Saw-Tooth Tower

TIMS Towers

TIMS Towers Data Table

Building	Volume Number of Cubes
Tall Tower	
Sky-High Tower	
Triple Double Tower	
Saw-Tooth Tower	

Two Towers

Find the volume of each tower.

Tower 1　　　　　　　　**Tower 2**

Volume = _____　　　Volume = _____

Which tower has the greater volume? _____

Which tower is taller? _____

Name _____ Date _____

TIMS Radio Tower

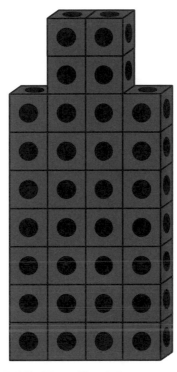

TIMS Radio Tower

Height = _____

Volume = _____

How did you find your answer?

_____

_____

_____

_____

Ruffy and the Snake

Front

Back

Side 1

Side 2

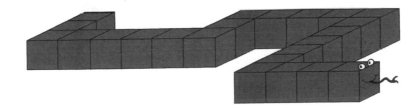

Name _____ Date _____

Comparing Ruffy and the Snake

Look at the different views on the *Ruffy and the Snake* Activity Page. Use these pictures to help you answer the questions below.

That's pretty amazing!

1. Who looks bigger, Ruffy or the snake? Explain your answer.

_____

_____

_____

_____

2. Work with a partner. Find the volume of Ruffy and the volume of the snake. You may build them with cubes.

Ruffy has a volume of _____.

The snake has a volume of _____.

Unit 13

Thinking About Addition and Subtraction

	Student Guide	Adventure Book	Unit Resource Guide*
Lesson 1			
Make Ten	●		●
Lesson 2			
Seeing Doubles	●		
Lesson 3			
Doubles and Halves	●		
Lesson 4			
Odd and Even Revisited	●		●
Lesson 5			
Problem Solving	●		

Unit Resource Guide pages are from the teacher materials.

Name _____ Date _____

Make Ten at Home

Dear Family Member:

Your child played the game *Make Ten* in school and is ready to teach it to someone at home. You may use the digit cards your child has brought home or use a deck of playing cards by removing the kings, queens, and jacks. The aces can represent the number 1. Have beans, toothpicks, or other small objects handy for your child to use in solving problems during the game. Also, please help your child keep a record of the number of people he or she teaches to play the game.

Tally marks are recorded in groups of five. Example: 8 tallies = |||| |||

Thank you.

Make a tally mark for each person you teach to play the game.

Tallies _____

Make a tally mark for every five minutes you play the game.

Tallies _____   Total minutes _____

Parent's signature _____

Child's signature _____

Return this sheet to school by _____.

Doubles Bulletin Board

Dear Family Member:

Your child is studying ways to represent doubling numbers in class.

Things that occur in pairs show doubles: twins, feet, gloves, and shoes. Help your child find or create a picture showing a double number, and help write a number sentence for the picture. An example number sentence for a picture of two feet would be 5 toes + 5 toes = 10 toes.

Thank you for your cooperation.

Draw or paste a cutout picture of a double. Write a number sentence for your double. Bring this page to school for our Doubles Board.

Name _____   Date _____

Doubles Problems

Think of two doubles. Draw a picture of the doubles for Question 1 and Question 2. Write a number sentence that fits each picture. Then, tell a story about each picture.

1.

_____ + _____ = _____

_____

_____

_____

2. Draw your second picture here. Write your number sentence and story in the spaces below.

_____ + _____ = _____

_____

_____

_____

_____

_____

Doubles Railroad

Players

This is a game for two players.

Materials

- *Doubles Railroad Game Board*
- 1 bean for each player
- clear plastic spinner or a pencil and paper clip
- 50 connecting cubes

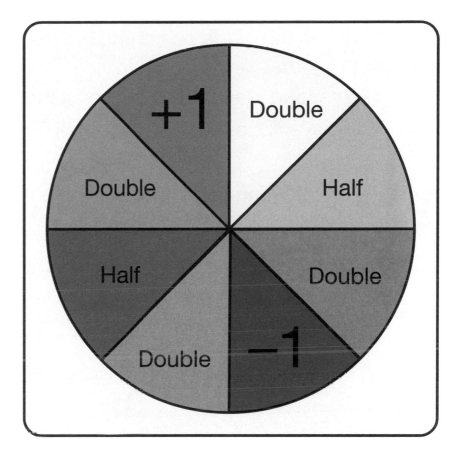

Rules

Spin to find your move:

Double: Move to the number that is double where your bean is now.

Half: Move to the number that is half of where your bean is now. (Your teacher will talk about what to do if your bean is on an odd number.)

+1: Move forward one space.

–1: Move back one space.

TURN PAGE for game directions.

Name _____ Date _____

1. Both players place their beans on 1 on the game board.

2. The first player spins. The player figures out where to move on the game board and moves. This completes his or her turn.

3. The second player spins and makes a move.

4. The player who reaches or passes 50 first wins the game.

Hint: Use connecting cubes to help figure out where to move.

Name _____ Date _____

Doubles Railroad Game Board

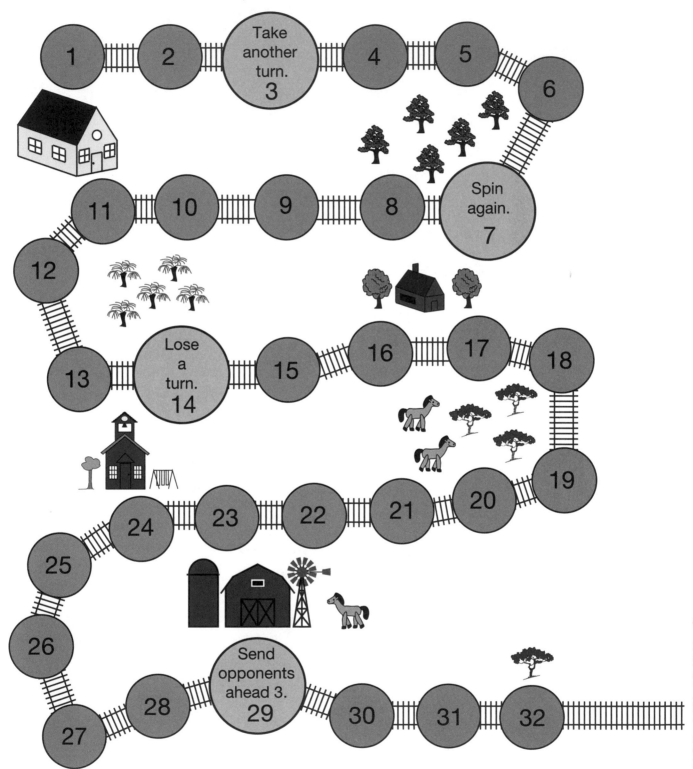

Name _____ Date _____

Train Yard

50
49
48
47
Lose a turn. 46
45
44
43
Spin again. 42
41
40
39
38
37
33
34
35
36

Doubles and Halves   SG • Grade 1 • Unit 13 • Lesson 3

Name _____ Date _____

Doubles Railroad at Home

Dear Family Member:

Your child played the game *Doubles Railroad* in school and is ready to teach it to someone at home. Have beans, toothpicks, or other small objects handy for your child to use in solving problems during the game. For example, to double 12, your child might make two stacks of 12 pennies. He or she might skip count by twos to find the total number of pennies.

Please help your child keep a record of the number of people he or she teaches to play the game. You can make a spinner by spinning a paper clip around a pencil.

Thank you for your help.

Make a tally mark for each person you teach to play the game.

Tallies _____

Make a tally mark for every five minutes you play the game.

Tallies _____   Total minutes _____

Parent's signature _____

Child's signature _____

Return this sheet to school by _____.

Doubles and Halves

Dear Family Member:

In class, your child used connecting cubes to double a number and to find half of a number. For example, to double 6, he or she built a tower with 6 cubes and then doubled it. Your child counted the total number of cubes to find how many cubes were in the new tower. Help your child double and halve the numbers in the table. Your child may use coins, toothpicks, beans, or other counters.

Thank you.

Number	The Number Doubled
6	12
10	
14	
17	

Number	Half of Number
8	
26	
38	

Problem Set

Solve the problems using ten frames, counters, mental math, or drawings. Show how you solved each one.

1. Marie had some dolls. She got 3 more for her birthday. Then she had 9 dolls. How many dolls did she have before her birthday?

2. Jessica had some toy cars. She gave 3 toy cars to Jim. Then she had 5. How many toy cars did she have before she gave 3 away?

3. In November, Ellen lost 3 teeth. She then had 12. How many teeth did she have to start with?

4. Jack had 12 raffle tickets. He sold some to his friends. He then had 8 tickets. How many raffle tickets did he sell?

Homework Problem Set

Solve the problems using counters, mental math, or drawings. Show how you solved each one.

1. Ruth had 7 stickers. Mrs. Rhoton gave her 3 more. How many did Ruth have in all?

2. Mo is 6 years old. Her sister Ann is 14 years old. How much older is Ann?

3. Beau has $2. He wants an action figure that costs $6. How much more money does he need?

4. Frank has 14 action figures. Three are bad guys. The rest are good guys. How many good guys does he have?

Milly and Billy's Data

Colors

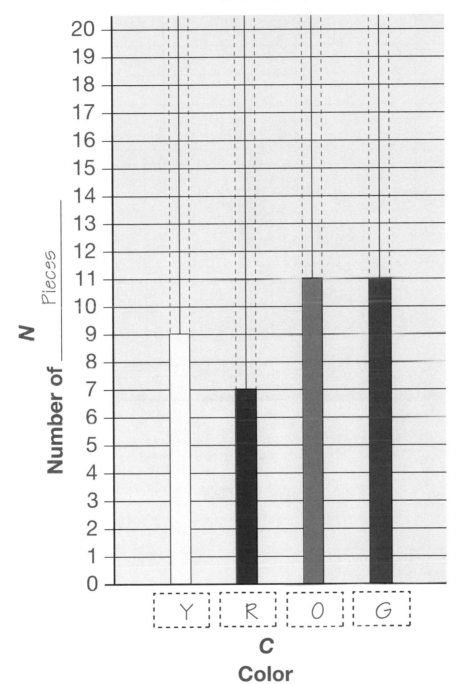

Y = yellow
R = red
O = orange
G = green

Name _____ Date _____

Rolling Along with Links

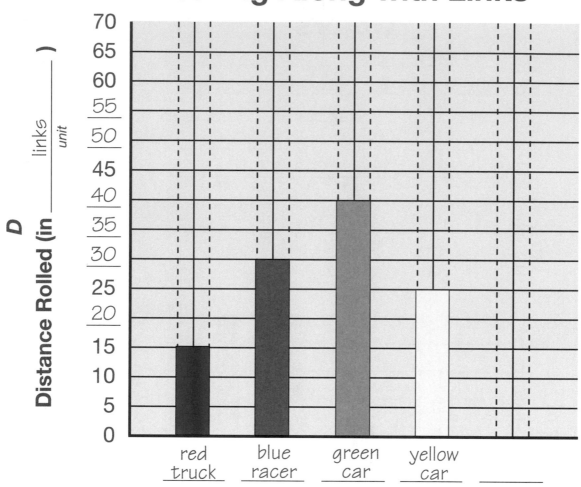

Distance Rolled (in $\frac{links}{unit}$) **D**

Type of Car **T**

Name _____ Date _____

More Problems

Solve the problems using ten frames, counters, mental math, or drawings.

1. Stephen has 9 pencils. Ishmael has 5 pencils. How many more pencils does Stephen have?

2. LaTonya has 5 pencils. Marty has 7 more pencils than LaTonya. How many pencils does Marty have?

3. Lauren has 12 books. There are 8 hardcover books. The rest of the books are paperbacks. How many paperbacks does she have?

4. Blanca had $8. She spent $3 on a book. How much money does she have left?

Name _____ Date _____

Recipe for Peanut Butter, Jelly, and Banana Sandwiches

For One Class

20 slices of bread   10 tablespoons of jelly

4 bananas   10 tablespoons of peanut butter

1. Pretend you need to serve sandwiches to two classes. How many of each ingredient will you need to double the recipe?

_____ slices of bread   _____ tablespoons of jelly

_____ bananas   _____ tablespoons of peanut butter

2. Pretend you need to serve sandwiches to only half the class. How many of each ingredient will you need to make only half the recipe?

_____ slices of bread   _____ tablespoons of jelly

_____ bananas   _____ tablespoons of peanut butter

Name _____ Date _____

How Many?

Solve the problems using ten frames, counters, mental math, or drawings. Show how you solved each one.

1. Maria has 4 goldfish and 6 angelfish. How many fish does she have?

2. Nick has 9 erasers. He has 5 more erasers than Jennifer. How many erasers does Jennifer have?

3. There were 12 birds on a wire. Then 3 flew away, looking for a tree. How many birds were left on the wire?

4. Eight fat frogs croaked really loud. More frogs came to make a crowd. Now, there are 12 frogs. How many came?

Exploring Multiplication and Division

	Student Guide	Adventure Book	Unit Resource Guide*
Lesson 1			
Math Mice	●		
Lesson 2			
Pets	●		
Lesson 3			
Problems That Will Knock Your Socks Off!	●		

Unit Resource Guide pages are from the teacher materials.

Squid Squares

These are squid squares. Study the first one. Then, make the other two look just like it.

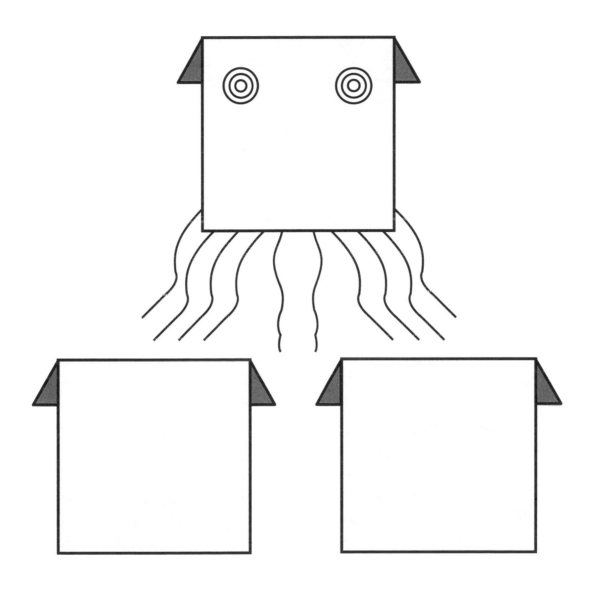

Name _____ Date _____

1. How many circles did you draw to make eyes for **one** squid?

2. How many circles did you draw to make eyes for **two** squid? Show how you know this.

3. How many arms did you draw for **two** squid? What number could you count by to help you?

4. If you saw **ten** eyes glowing deep in the sea, how many squid would there be? Show a way you might figure this out.

Math Mice

Name _____   Date _____

Counting Pets

Dear Family Member:

In class, we are looking at the types of pets students own. We are using the information to create number problems. In this homework assignment, we ask your child to count the number of pets in your household as well as those in another household. Your child will write number problems using the data. If there are no pets in your household, please help your child get this information from two other households that have at least one pet.

Here is the first row of a sample chart.

Family Name	Dog	Cat	Fish	Turtle	Bird	Other
Smith		1	5			

Sample number problem: How many more fish are there than cats in the Smith family?

Thank you for your cooperation.

Family Name	Dog	Cat	Fish	Turtle	Bird	Other

Name _____ Date _____

Write five number problems that use your data. Show how you solved each problem.

1. _____

_____

2. _____

_____

3. _____

_____

4. _____

_____

5. _____

_____

Room 222's Pets Graph

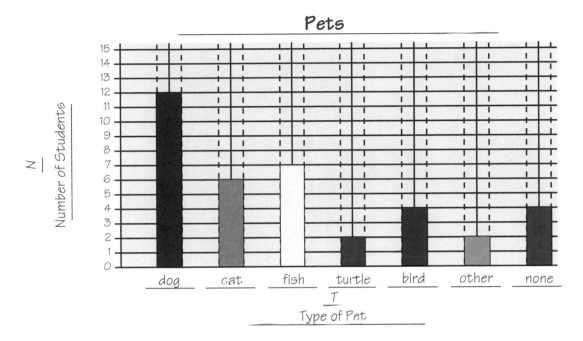

1. What is the most common pet? _____ _____

2. What is the least common pet? _____ _____

3. **A.** How many students have cats? _____

   B. Which pet is owned by double that number?

   _____

4. **A.** How many students have turtles, birds, and fish?

   _____

   B. Are there more students with dogs than turtles, birds,

   and fish together? _____

5. Tell a story you see in the graph. ————————————

————————————————————————————

————————————————————————————

————————————————————————————

More Pet Problems

Answer the questions. Show your work with a picture or number sentence.

1. Imagine that you keep six birds in one cage. How many wings are in the cage?

2. Imagine you have 15 turtles. There are 3 rocks in your tank. The same number of turtles sit on each rock. How many turtles need to share each rock?

Animal Shelter

Answer the questions. Show your work.

Maria, José, Juan, Celina, and Angela are brothers and sisters. Their mother told them they can adopt a puppy from an animal shelter. But first, they must save $45. The children want to be fair. They must each save the same amount of money.

1. How much money does each child need to save?

2. The children adopted a puppy they named Rex. They bought Rex a collar that cost $10. Each child paid the same amount. How much money did each child spend on the collar?

The Old Woman and Her Cats

Answer the questions. Show your work in words or pictures on another piece of paper.

There was an old woman who wore pretty hats.
Within her house, she kept many cats.
Of love, they had plenty, but food they did need.
With each bowl of food, three cats she could feed.

She had nine large bowls, all ready to use.
But the bowls and the cats she began to confuse.
"Do I have enough bowls? Can I feed every cat?
Can somebody please help me figure out that?"

1. How many cats can
    the woman feed using
    nine bowls?

2. **A.** If she had 25 cats, how many bowls would she need?

    B. Would she have room at the bowls for more cats?

Problems That Will Knock Your Socks Off!

Animal Boots

A farmer wants to buy boots for his animals. The farmer has horses and chickens. How many boots will he need to buy?

Animals	Number of Boots
(5 horses)	20
(3 horses)	
(7 chickens)	
(4 chickens)	
(2 horses, 3 chickens)	
	18

Is there another answer to the last row? Draw a picture to show your idea.

Name _____ Date _____

Basil the Basset Hound

Answer the questions. Show your work in words or pictures.

1. Basil is a basset hound. He had 23 bones buried in his yard. One weekend, he dug up 12 of them. How many bones are still buried?

2. Basil and his three buddies found 16 bones. They agreed to share them equally. How many bones did each dog get?

3. It was Basil's lucky day! His owner made a roast that had two bones in it. Basil wished his owner would make the same kind of roast every day for a week. How many bones would Basil have if his owner granted his wish?

Exploring 3-D Shapes

	Student Guide	Adventure Book	Unit Resource Guide*
Daily Practice and Problems			
The Boy Who Traveled to Find a Hard Problem I	●		●
Lesson 1			
Tubes, Boxes, Spheres, and Cubes	●		
Lesson 2			
Sizing Cylinders	●		●
Lesson 3			
Looking at Prisms	●		
Lesson 4			
In the Shapes Kitchen			

Unit Resource Guide pages are from the teacher materials.

The Boy Who Traveled to Find a Hard Problem I

Once there was a man who had a daughter and a son. The children were clever and hard-working.

The son could never understand when people said, "I can't figure that out. It's a hard problem." He always knew the answer right away.

Dinner Guests

One evening, the family had some dinner guests. The father wanted to set the table. He said, "There are four of us in the family, and we have three guests. How many plates do we need?"

Show your work here.

The family needs _____ plates.

Shepherd

The boy set out from home in search of a hard problem. Soon he came to a shepherd who was sitting with 18 sheep by the roadside. The poor shepherd was crying. The boy asked what the matter was.

The shepherd said, "I have a really hard problem. I am watching 18 sheep for Farmer Bigshoe and Farmer Digdeep. I know that Bigshoe gave me 12 sheep, but I'll never figure out how many Digdeep gave me: It's too hard!"

Show your work here.

Digdeep gave the shepherd _____ sheep.

Daily Practice and Problems

Ducks

Soon he came upon two women arguing over ducks. The boy asked what was wrong. One woman said, "I had 5 ducks and some of her ducks flew over here. Now, there are 13 ducks here, and we don't know how many are hers. What a hard problem!"

Show your work here.

_____ ducks flew over here.

[To be continued in the next unit.]

Name _____

Date _____

Describe That Shape

Test what each shape can do. Record your findings in the table below. Can you think of other words to describe these shapes? Write those words in the bottom row.

	Cylinders (Tubes)	Prisms (Boxes)	Cubes	Spheres (Balls)
This shape can roll.				
This shape can stack.				
This shape can slide.				

Name _____ Date _____

Cylinder Search

Dear Family Member:

In class, your child explored three-dimensional shapes. I have asked your child to find everyday objects that have a cylindrical shape and to record them in the data table on the back of this page. (Your child should write in the column headings on the blank table as shown below.) Objects like empty soup cans are good examples of cylinders because they have circular ends and parallel straight sides. Some objects like most paper cups are almost cylinders, but their sides are not quite straight.

After your child has completed the data table, he or she should bring three to five of the cylinders to school. Students will use these objects in a class activity. Please help your child find and select light, non-breakable examples that have circular ends and straight sides to bring to school for this activity.

Thank you for your help.

Search for objects that have a cylinder shape, like the toilet paper core. Then, record the names of the cylinder shapes you see at your home. Make the headings in your data table look like the ones below.

Cylinder Shape	Almost Cylinder Shape

Choose three to five items from your data table to bring to school.

Name _____ Date _____

Tubes, Boxes, Spheres, and Cubes

Sorting Cylinders

Your team will work together to sort cylinders.

Directions

1. Use a copy of *Categories for Sorting Cylinders*. Cut out the names of the three categories:

    A. **Height Longer** than the Circumference

    B. **Circumference Longer** than the Height

    C. **Same** Circumference and Height

2. Make a prediction. Which group will have the greatest number of cylinders?

    _____

3. Compare the height and circumference of each cylinder. Use string.

4. Sort the cylinders. Place each cylinder in the correct group.

Name _____ Date _____

5. Record the results on the Cylinders Data Table.

Cylinders Data Table

Categories of Cylinders	Number of Cylinders
Height Longer than the Circumference	
Circumference Longer than the Height	
Same Circumference and Height	

Total number of cylinders measured: _____

Sizing Cylinders

Box Collection

Dear Family Member:

In school, we will study boxes to learn about the properties of cubes and rectangular prisms (boxes). I have asked your child to look at home for boxes to use in a class activity. Please help your child find and select one or two boxes to bring to school.

Thank you.

Our class needs a box collection. Look at home for one or two boxes to bring to school tomorrow.

Here are a few examples:

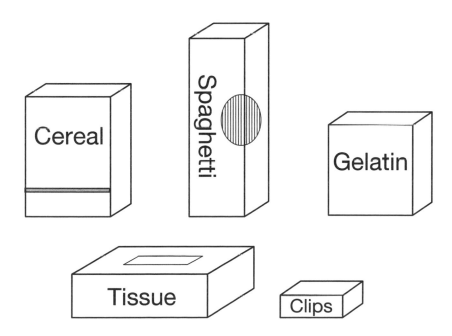

Find the Shapes

Two construction workers are having lunch. There are many different shapes in the picture below.

Color all the shapes you can find with the colors listed below:
- **Blue for cylinders.**
- **Red for rectangular prisms.**
- **Green for spheres.**
- **Circle all the cubes with** orange.

3-D Shapes

Cut out the pictures. Paste them under their names. Then describe each shape.

1. **Cylinder**

2. **Cube**

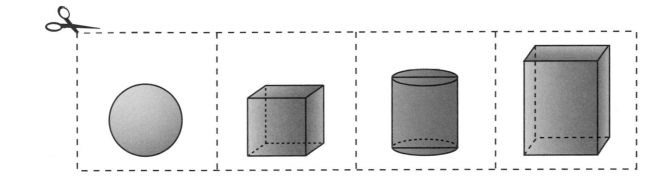

3. Prism

_____

_____

_____

_____

_____

4. Sphere

_____

_____

_____

_____

_____

Sphere Search

Homework

Dear Family Member:

In class, your child has explored various three-dimensional shapes. I have asked your child to find everyday objects at home that have a spherical (ball) shape. Your child should record his or her findings in the data table on the back of this page. Please help your child find examples.

I have also asked your child to bring food ads to school. I am most interested in ads that show pictures or drawings of food containers, such as boxes and cans, or produce, such as oranges and cucumbers. As a class activity, your child will create a book with cutouts of these geometric shapes.

Thank you for your cooperation.

Search for objects that have a sphere shape. Then record the names of the sphere shapes you see in your home. Use the data table on the back of this page. Make the headings in your data table look like the ones below.

Sphere Shape	Almost Sphere Shape

Bring food ads to school.

Name _____ Date _____

Looking at Prisms

Collecting and Organizing Data

	Student Guide	Adventure Book	Unit Resource Guide*
Daily Practice and Problems			
The Boy Who Traveled to Find a Hard Problem II	●		●
Lesson 1			
The Martians	●	●	
Lesson 2			
Food Sort	●		
Lesson 3			
Healthy Kids	●		

Unit Resource Guide pages are from the teacher materials.

The Boy Who Traveled to Find a Hard Problem II Gold Pieces

The boy who traveled to find a hard problem went to town. He found the king sitting in his counting house scratching his head. The king said, "Who are you? Can you help me? I have 39 gold pieces, but I need to pay the army 57 gold pieces. I can't figure out how many more gold pieces I need."

Show your work here.

The king needs _____ more gold pieces.

Royal Rabbits

Next, the king and the boy went to the royal rabbit hutch. The king said, "I had some rabbits before, but 15 new ones have been born. Now, there are 55 rabbits. My problem is that I don't know how many I started with. If you can solve this problem for me, I will reward you with a bird that lays golden eggs."

Show your work here.

The king started with _____ rabbits.

Home Again

The boy thanked the king for the bird and set out for home. When he got there, everybody was happy to have him back. They were also happy to have the golden bird.

The family was rich now, and everyone was very content, especially the boy. He could think of lots of hard problems about the bird and the golden eggs. **Write one problem below.**

_____

_____

_____

Favorite Foods

Homework

Dear Family Member:

Please help your child record his or her favorite foods in preparation for conducting a food survey.

Thank you for your help.

List ten of your favorite foods.

1. _____

2. _____

3. _____

4. _____

5. _____

6. _____

7. _____

8. _____

9. _____

10. _____

Food Group Sort 1

You will need your *Favorite Foods* Homework Page. Sort your favorite foods into these six food groups. Write the names of your favorite foods in the boxes below.

Grains (includes bread, cereal, rice, and pasta)	Milk (also includes yogurt and cheese)
Vegetables	Meat and Beans (also includes poultry, fish, eggs, and nuts)
Fruits	Oils, Fats, and Sweets

Food Group Sort 2

Sort the foods below into these six food groups. Write the number of the group after each food. Some foods are in more than one group.

Food Groups

1. **Grains (includes bread, cereal, rice, and pasta)**
2. **Vegetables**
3. **Fruits**
4. **Milk (also includes yogurt and cheese)**
5. **Meat and Beans (also includes poultry, fish, eggs, and nuts)**
6. **Oils, Fats, and Sweets**

french fries ____

corn on the cob ____

pineapple ____

ice cream ____

orange juice ____

grapes ____

hamburger ____

rice and beans ____

corn flakes ____

boiled egg ____

chicken taco ____

yogurt ____

hot cocoa ____

shrimp ____

pizza ____

carrots ____

chili ____

peanut butter sandwich ____

Name _____ Date _____

Joni's and Bobbie's Breakfasts

Joni eats the same breakfast every day. She eats rice puffs, milk, slices of apples, banana bread, and orange juice.

Bobbie eats the same breakfast every day also. She eats a waffle with strawberries, whipped cream, and maple syrup. With it she has bacon and a glass of milk.

Help them find out what food groups their breakfast foods belong to. Write the number(s) of the food group(s) after each food.

Joni's Breakfast	**Bobbie's Breakfast**
rice puffs _____	waffle _____
milk _____	strawberries _____
slices of apples _____	whipped cream _____
banana bread _____	maple syrup _____
orange juice _____	bacon _____
	milk _____

1. Grains	4. Milk
2. Vegetables	5. Meat and Beans
3. Fruits	6. Oils, Fats, and Sweets

Name _____ Date _____

I Ate That!

Homework

Dear Family Member:

Please help your child gather data about everything he or she eats during the course of one day. Use the guidelines on the back to help your child record his or her daily servings in each food group. It is not important that measurements be precise. If a combination food needs to be recorded, such as a hamburger with toppings, simply record a tally mark in the box for each of the major food groups that can be seen easily. We won't collect data on the oil group. Most Americans get enough oil in the food they eat.

Please complete this full-day data collection beginning the morning of _____ .

Thank you.

Use a tally mark to record one serving of each type of food eaten.

Food Group	Breakfast	Lunch	Dinner	Snacks	Total
Grains					
Vegetables					
Fruits					
Milk					
Meat and Beans					
Fats and Sweets					

Name _____ Date _____

Recommended amounts for children 4–8 years old, according to the U.S. Department of Agriculture.

Servings

Food Group	Servings	Serving Size for Selected Food Items
Grains	4–5	• 1 slice of bread, 1 tortilla, or $\frac{1}{2}$ pita • $\frac{1}{2}$ hamburger bun, English muffin, or bagel • $\frac{1}{2}$ cup cooked cereal, rice, or pasta • 1 cup ready-to-eat breakfast cereal
Vegetables	3	• $\frac{1}{2}$ cup cut-up raw or cooked vegetables • $\frac{1}{2}$ cup vegetable juice • 1 cup leafy raw vegetables, such as lettuce, greens, or spinach
Fruits	3	• a whole fruit, such as medium apple, banana, or orange • $\frac{1}{2}$ grapefruit • $\frac{1}{2}$ cup of juice • $\frac{1}{2}$ cup of berries • $\frac{1}{2}$ cup canned fruit • $\frac{1}{4}$ cup dried fruit
Milk	2	• 1 cup milk • 1 cup yogurt • $1\frac{1}{2}$ ounces natural cheese • 2 ounces processed cheese
Meat and Beans	3–4	• 1 ounce of lean meat, poultry, or fish • $\frac{1}{2}$ ounce nuts or seeds • 1 egg or $\frac{1}{4}$ cup tofu • 1 tablespoon peanut butter • $\frac{1}{4}$ cup cooked beans
Oils	4 tsp.* *Most Americans get enough oil in the food they eat.	These foods are mostly oil: • soft margarine • salad dressing • mayonnaise • vegetable oil These foods contain oil: • nuts • peanut butter • avocados • fish
Extra Fats and Sweets	Limit your amount	• candy bar • butter, stick margarine • ice cream • bacon, fat from meat • cakes, cookies • soda, fruit drinks

Healthy Kids

Healthy Kids

Draw a picture of the experiment.

Record what you eat for one day on the *I Ate That!* Homework Pages.

Name _____ Date _____

I Ate That! Graph

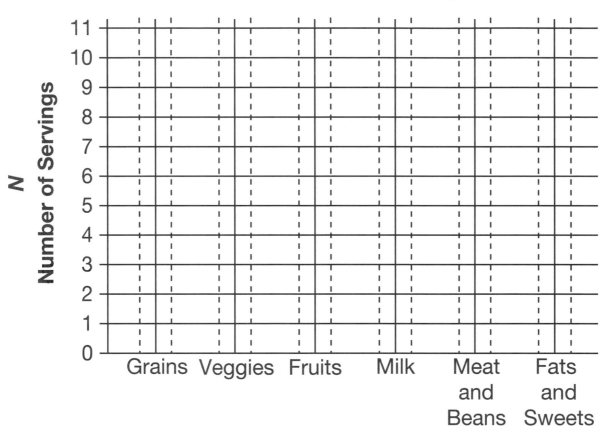

Number of Servings *N*

G
Food Group

1. Look at the recommended amounts in the Servings Table. How does what you ate compare to what you should be eating? Are there things you should change? Are there things you should keep the same?

2. Think about eating better beginning today. How would you like your graph to look? Show it on the graph below.

Healthier Kids

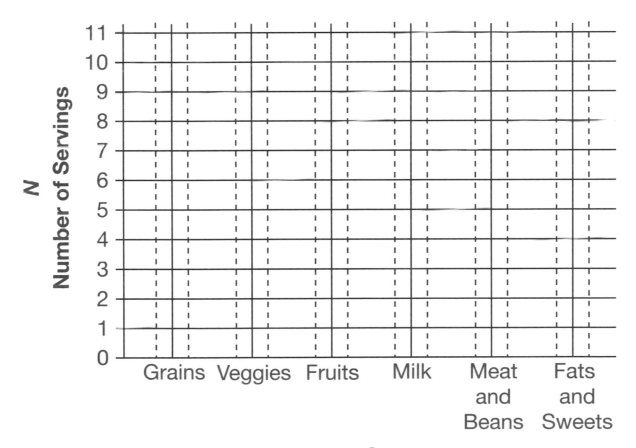

N
Number of Servings

G
Food Group

David's and Cindy's Food

1. David and Cindy recorded the servings they ate in one day. Find the total for each food group.

David's Data Table

Food Group	Tallies	Total
Grains	|||	
Vegetables	||/	
Fruits	||/	
Milk	|||	
Meat and Beans	||/	
Fats and Sweets	||/	

Cindy's Data Table

Food Group	Tallies	Total
Grains	||	
Vegetables	|||/	
Fruits	||/	
Milk	|	
Meat and Beans	||/	
Fats and Sweets	|	

2. Compare the data in David's and Cindy's data tables.

   A. Who ate more servings of grains? How much more?

   _____

   _____

   _____

   B. Who ate more servings of food in one day? How many more servings?

   _____

   _____

   _____

   C. Make up your own problem that uses the two data tables. Then show how to find the answer.

   _____

   _____

   _____

   _____

Healthy Kids

3. Transfer the data from David's data table to David's graph.

David's Graph

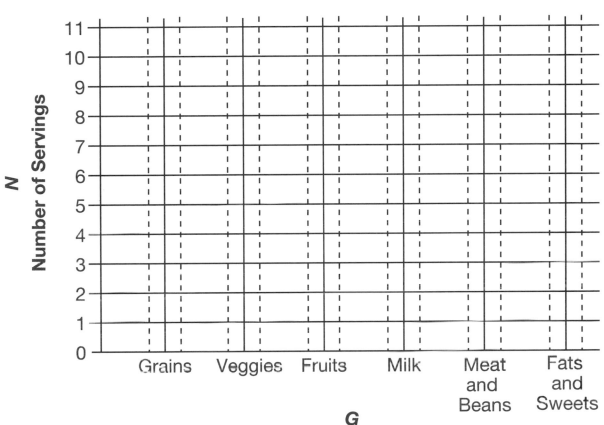

4. Tell the story of David's graph. What do you think about David's diet?

- What should he keep the same? _____

_____

- What should he change? _____

_____

Moving Beyond 100

	Student Guide	Adventure Book	Unit Resource Guide*
Lesson 1			
Tensland		⬤	
Lesson 2			
Our Class in Tensland	⬤		
Lesson 3			
Counting One Hundred Seventy-two	⬤		
Lesson 4			
Adding Hundreds	⬤		

Unit Resource Guide pages are from the teacher materials.

At School in Tensland

In another class, students are also collecting buttons.
J.D. has circled his buttons to help count them.

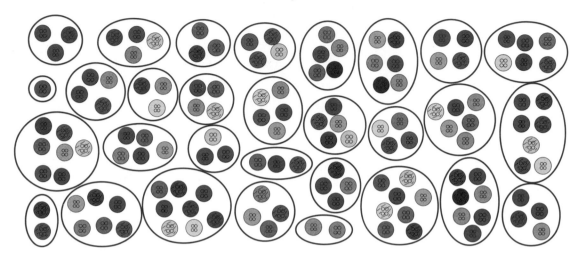

Jonay has organized her buttons, too.

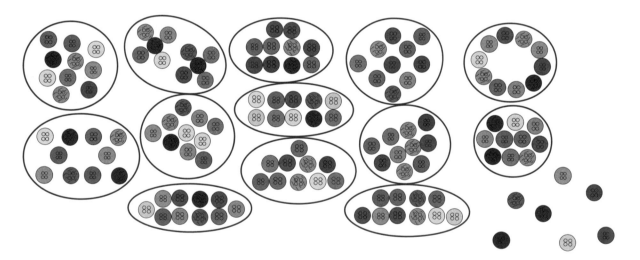

1. Whose buttons would you rather count:
   J.D.'s buttons or Jonay's buttons? _____

2. Explain why you picked that group to count.

   _____

3. How many buttons are in the group you counted? _____

Name _____ Date _____

At Home in Tensland

Dear Family Member:

At school, your child has been working on counting and grouping large numbers of objects. Help your child share with you what he or she has learned. Please provide your child with a large number (more than 100 but fewer than 200) of objects to count. Some suggestions for objects: toothpicks, paper clips, macaroni, beans, small screws, washers, hex nuts, or pennies. Also, have small cups or containers available for sorting. Your child will then illustrate how the objects were counted and record the total number.

Thank you for your cooperation.

Report on what you counted at home:

1. The kind of objects I counted at home were:

   _____

2. My drawing below shows how I counted the objects.

3. I write that number of objects as _____

Copyright © Kendall/Hunt Publishing Company

Terry in Tensland

Terry also visited Tensland. He met a bunch of beans. They wanted help to get organized. Terry put them into groups of two to make them easier to count.

Terry counted 116 beans.

1. Do you agree with his count? _____

2. Tell Terry how to organize the beans another way.

_____

Name _____ Date _____

Pumpkin Patch

Counting One Hundred Seventy-two

SG • Grade 1 • Unit 17 • Lesson 3

Name _____ Date _____

Silvia and Douglas went pumpkin picking in the pumpkin patch. Silvia wondered how many pumpkins there were in all.

Count the number of pumpkins. Draw a picture showing how you counted the number of pumpkins. Then, tell your strategies.

_____

_____

_____

_____

_____

Counting One Hundred Seventy-two

Adding Numbers

Solve the following problems.

Set 1

$7 + 2 =$ _____ $70 + 20 =$ _____ $700 + 200 =$ _____

Set 2

$$\begin{array}{r} 6 \\ +3 \\ \hline \end{array}$$
$$\begin{array}{r} 60 \\ +30 \\ \hline \end{array}$$
$$\begin{array}{r} 600 \\ +300 \\ \hline \end{array}$$

Set 3

$$\begin{array}{r} 3 \\ +3 \\ \hline \end{array}$$
$$\begin{array}{r} 30 \\ +30 \\ \hline \end{array}$$
$$\begin{array}{r} 300 \\ +300 \\ \hline \end{array}$$

More Adding Numbers

Solve each set of problems below. Then, share your work with a family member.

Set 1

$4 + 3 =$ _____ $40 + 30 =$ _____ $400 + 300 =$ _____

Set 2

```
    5              50             500
  + 3            + 30           + 300
  ___            ____           _____
```

Set 3

```
    6              60             600
    1              10             100
  + 2            + 20           + 200
  ___            ____           _____
```

Pieces, Parts, and Symmetry

	Student Guide	Adventure Book	Unit Resource Guide*
Lesson 1			
Fold and Color	●		
Lesson 2			
Equal and Unequal	●		●
Lesson 3			
Fraction Puzzles	●		
Lesson 4			
A Class Full of Fractions	●		
Lesson 5			
Fraction Finale	●		

*Unit Resource Guide pages are from the teacher materials.

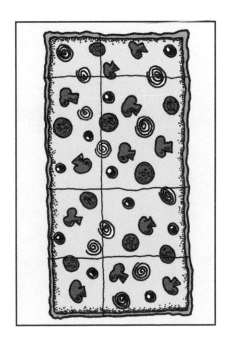

Fold and Color 1

Cut out the shapes below. Use them for the *Folding and Showing Halves* Activity Pages.

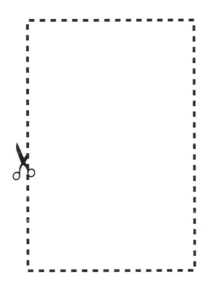

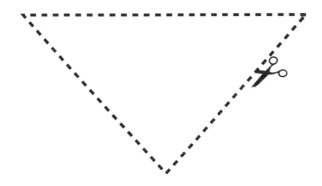

Folding and Showing Halves

Cut out the shapes on the *Fold and Color 1* Activity Page. Fold each shape in half. Color one-half of each shape. Paste the cutouts on the shapes below. Then, complete the sentence for each shape.

Daniel cut out a hexagon.
He folded it in half.
He colored one-half.

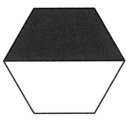

I colored ____$\frac{1}{2}$____ of

this ____hexagon____.

1. I colored _____ of

this _____.

2. I colored _____ of

this _____.

Name _____ Date _____

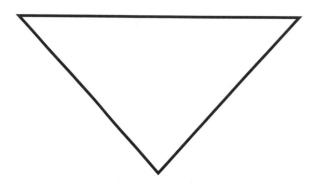 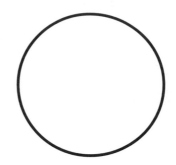

3. I colored _____ of

this _____.

4. I colored _____ of

this _____.

Fold and Color 2

Cut out the shapes below. Use them for the *Folding and Showing Fourths* Activity Pages.

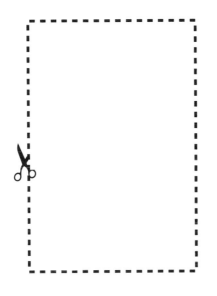

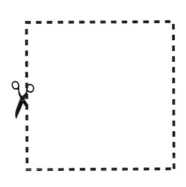

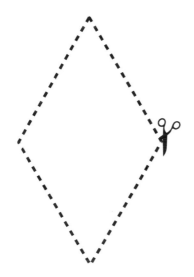

Folding and Showing Fourths

Use the shapes from the *Fold and Color 2* Activity Page. Fold each shape. Color one-fourth of each shape. Paste the cutouts on the shapes. Complete the sentence for each shape.

Daniel cut out a hexagon.
He folded it in fourths.
He colored one-fourth.

I colored ___$\frac{1}{4}$___ of

this ____hexagon____.

1. I colored _____ of

   this _____.

2. I colored _____ of

   this _____.

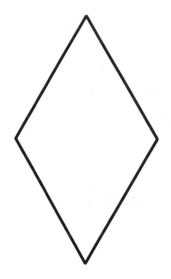

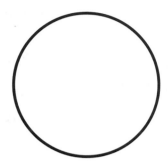

3. I colored _____ of

this _____.

4. I colored _____ of

this _____.

Copyright © Kendall/Hunt Publishing Company

Halves and Fourths in My Home

Homework

Dear Family Member:

In class today, we explored halves and fourths. Please help your child look at home for six items that come in halves or fourths. Some suggestions follow:

- A cracker might be scored to break easily into halves or fourths.

- Milk is packaged in one-half gallon and one-fourth gallon (quart) containers.

- One pound of butter or margarine is often divided into one-quarter pound sticks.

If your child cannot find six items, help him or her complete the list below by adding items, such as paper towels or napkins, that can easily be folded or cut in halves or fourths. If possible, have your child bring one example to school to share with the class.

Thank you for your help.

Look around your home for six items that come in fourths or halves. Make a list of them below.

1. _____   2. _____

3. _____   4. _____

5. _____   6. _____

Halves and Fourths

Use a green crayon to color all the drawings that show halves. Use a yellow crayon to color all the drawings that show fourths. Use a red crayon to trace the lines of symmetry you see. You might not color all of the shapes.

1. 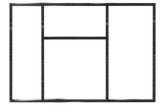   2.   3.

4. 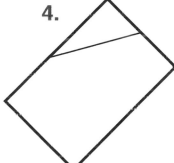   5. 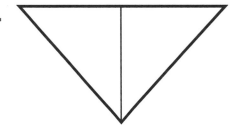   6.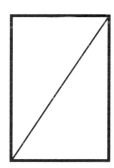

8.

7. 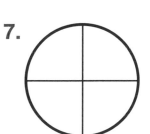   9.   10.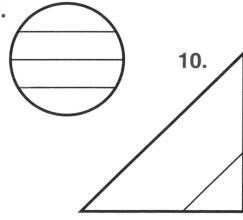

Name _____   Date _____

To Halve and to Halve Not

Equal and Unequal

To Fourth and to Fourth Not

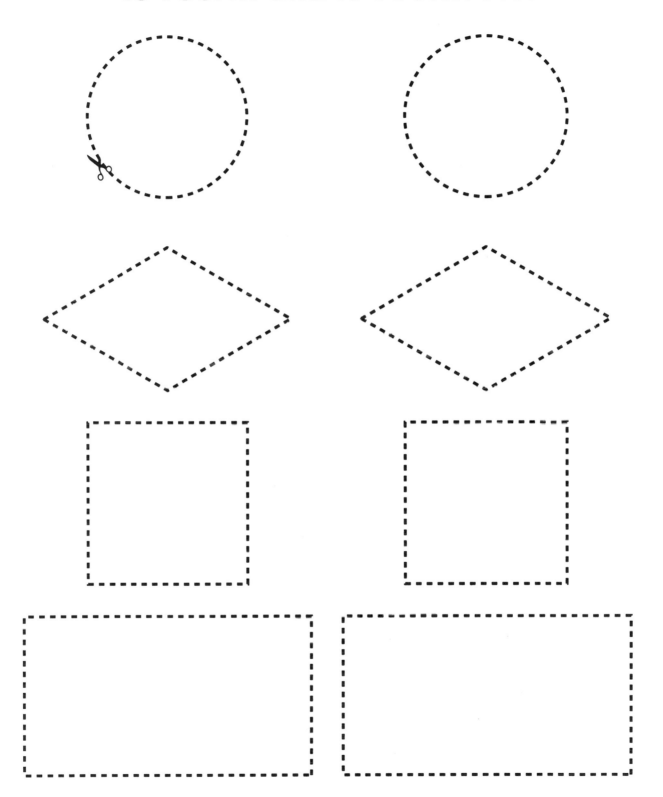

Name _____ Date _____

Circles and Ovals

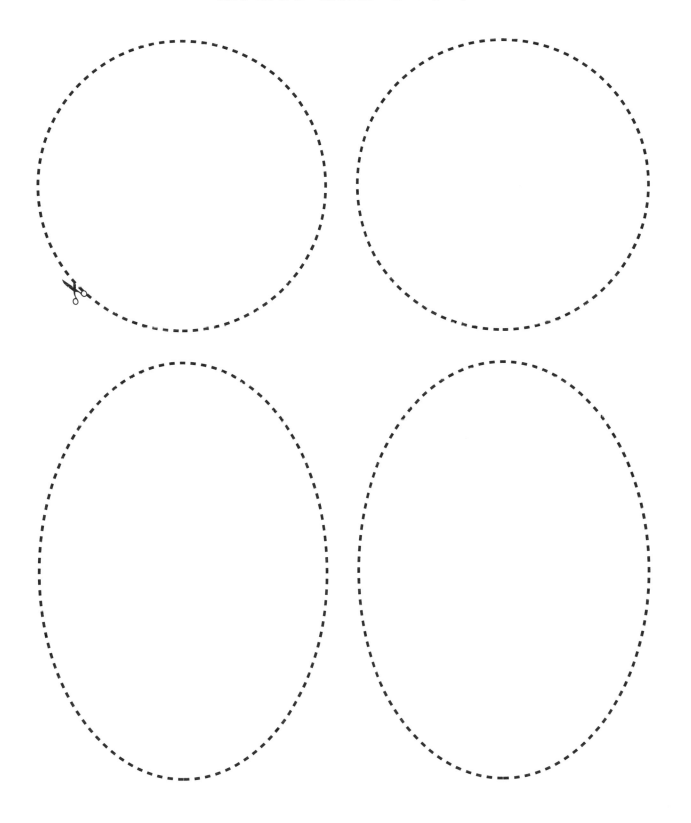

Name _____ Date _____

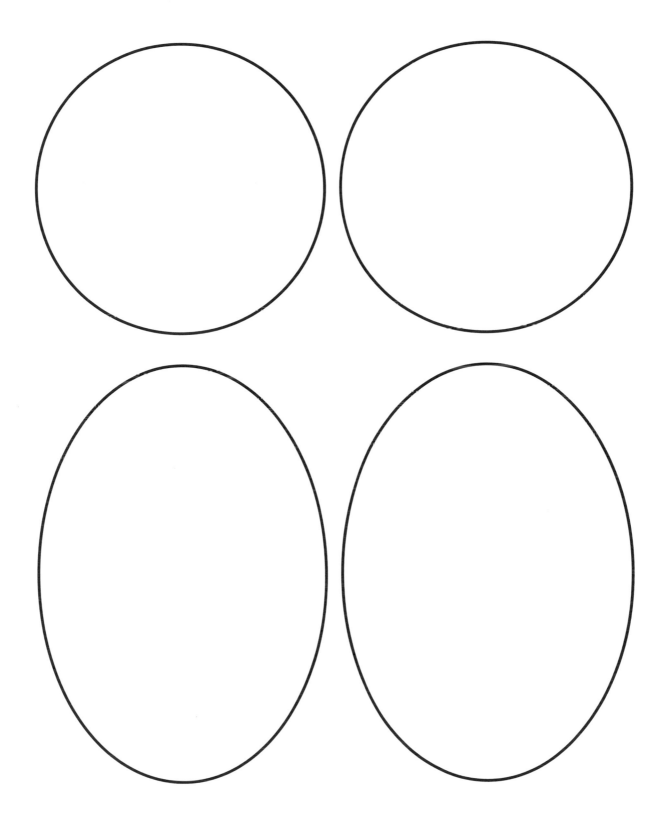

Rectangles and Squares

Name _____ Date _____

Find the Missing Half or Fourth

Draw a line from the whole to its half or fourth.

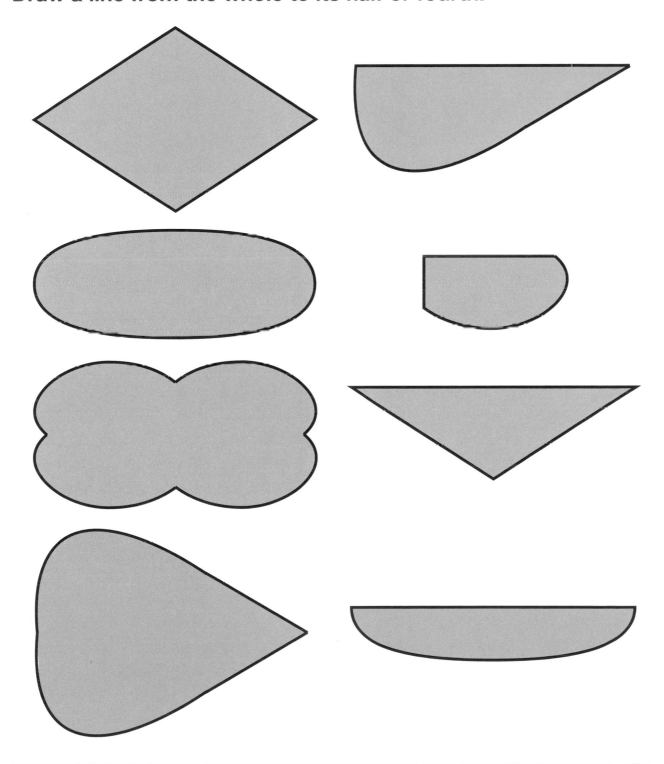

Which Shape Is It?

Complete each sentence below. Write the correct fraction and letter of the shape.

Is it $\frac{1}{2}$ or $\frac{1}{4}$ of shape A, B, C, or D?

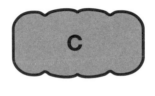
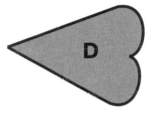

A   B   C   D

1. This is _____ of

   shape _____.

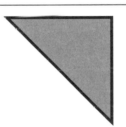

2. This is _____ of

   shape _____.

3. This is _____ of

   shape _____.

4. This is _____ of

   shape _____.

Drawing Fractions

1. Color the picture. Show that **one-third** of the children are wearing red shirts.

2. Add to the picture. Show that **three-eighths** of the dogs have bones.

Name _____   Date _____

3. Add to the picture. Show that **two-sixths** of the children are wearing boots.

4. What **fraction** of the kittens below have bowls?

_____

Pieces of Eighths

Jerome wanted to share a pizza with seven friends. He said, "I will cut the pizza into eighths. I will make eight pieces." This picture shows how Jerome's pizza looked when he finished.

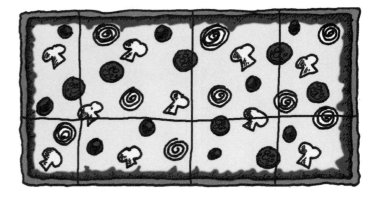

1. Tell what you think about the way Jerome cut the pizza. Did he cut the pizza into eighths?

   _____

   _____

   _____

2. Show how you would divide the pizza fairly among eight children.

Measurement and Mapping

	Student Guide	Adventure Book	Unit Resource Guide*
Lesson 1			
Meet Mr. Origin and Mr. Origin's Map	●		
Lesson 2			
Mr. Origin Left/Right	●		
Lesson 3			
Buried Treasure		●	

Unit Resource Guide pages are from the teacher materials.

Mr. Origin's Map and Data Table

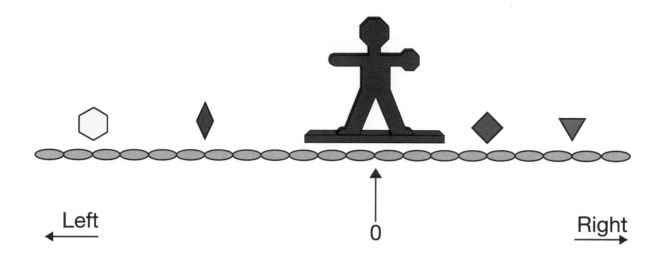

Left ←

0

Right →

Mr. Origin's Data Table

Object	Distance (in <u>links</u>) unit	Direction
triangle ▼	7	Right
square ◆		
rhombus ◆	6	
hexagon ⬡		

Mr. Origin Says

Homework

Dear Family Member:

In class today, we used a plastic figure called Mr. Origin to help develop skills with the directions right/left and front/back. Your child would like to share this learning experience with you. The hand with the mitten is Mr. Origin's right hand. The button shows that we are looking at Mr. Origin's front side. Help your child cut out Mr. Origin below. Then, follow the directions and play *Mr. Origin Says* with your child. Thank you.

Rules

1. Cut out Mr. Origin. Make sure the mitten on Mr. Origin's right hand is easy to see.

2. Decide who will be Mr. Origin—you or your family member.

3. One player makes a statement such as, "The refrigerator is to my right."

4. The Mr. Origin player moves Mr. Origin to make the statement true.

5. Reverse roles after you play a few rounds.

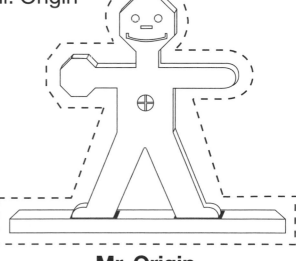

Mr. Origin

Here are a few more statements you might use to get started.

Mr. Origin says, "The chair is below me."

Mr. Origin says, "The door is in front of me."

Mr. Origin says, "The stove is to my right."

Now you are ready to play *Mr. Origin Says!*

Mr. Origin Left/Right

Work with your group. Find the distance and direction of each shape from Mr. Origin. Put your data in the table below. Label which setup your group used.

Mr. Origin Left/Right Data Table

Setup _____

Object	Distance (in _____) *unit*	Direction
triangle ▼		
square ◆		
rhombus ◆		
hexagon ⬡		

Name _____ Date _____

Map

Make a map of your Mr. Origin lab setup. Number the line by 2s. Then, show the

location of the objects. Put a T for 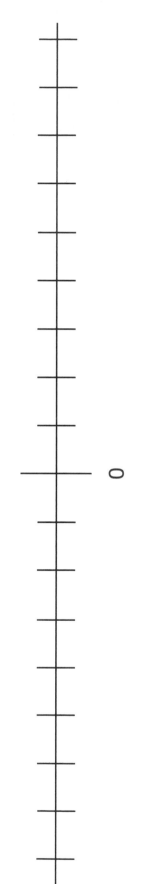**, an S for** **, an R for** **, and an H for** 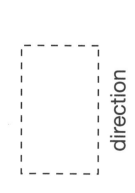 **.**

0

┌ ─ ─ ┐
│   │
│   │
└ ─ ─ ┘
direction

_____
unit

┌ ─ ─ ┐
│   │
│   │
└ ─ ─ ┘
direction

Explore

To answer Questions 1–4 use your setup or your map.

1. What object is farthest from Mr. Origin? _____

2. How far is it from Mr. Origin? _____

3. What direction is it from Mr. Origin? _____

4. **Use your setup.** How far is the rhombus from the triangle?

   _____

5. **Use your map.** Find the distance between the rhombus and the triangle in links. Explain how you got your answer.

   _____

   _____

   _____

6. **Use your map.** How far is the square from the hexagon in links?

   _____

7. **Use your setup.** Measure the distance between the square and the hexagon with links. Record your answer.

   _____

Thinking about Mr. Origin

Jan has a Mr. Origin on her desk. She uses links to measure distances.

hex nut   spool   penny

1. Mark the location of each object. Use a dot on the line below.
   - Put **HN** by the dot for hex nut.
   - Put **S** by the dot for spool.
   - Put **P** by the dot for penny.

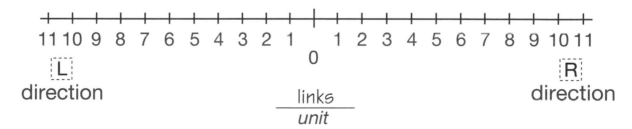

11 10 9 8 7 6 5 4 3 2 1   1 2 3 4 5 6 7 8 9 10 11

0

L
direction

links
unit

R
direction

2. How far is the center of the hex nut from the center of

   the spool? _____

Name _____ Date _____

Here is Juan's map.

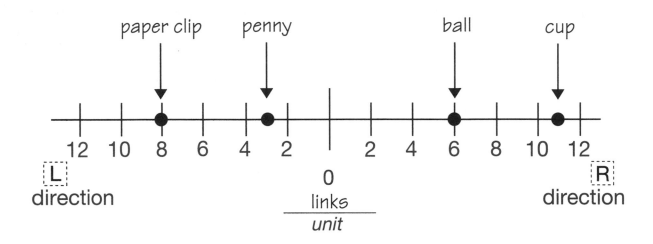

3. How far is the penny from the ball? _____

4. Fill in the data table using Juan's map.

Object	Distance (in _____) unit	Direction
paper clip		
penny		
ball		
cup		

Vanessa Finds Her Money

Vanessa does a Mr. Origin activity. This is her map.

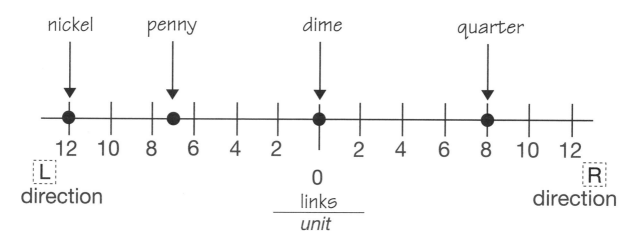

Fill in the data table.

Vanessa's Data Table

Object	Distance (in ____) unit	Direction

1. How far is the nickel from the quarter? _____

2. How far is the penny from the nickel? _____

Looking Back at First Grade

	Student Guide	Adventure Book	Unit Resource Guide*
Lesson 1			
Problem Solving	●		
Lesson 2			
End-of-Year Test			●

Unit Resource Guide pages are from the teacher materials.

Problem-Solving Problems 1–21

Problem 1

Complete the following part-part-whole problems. Write a number sentence for each one.

Part 5	Part 3
Whole	

Part 50	Part
Whole 80	

Part	Part 300
Whole 800	

_____ _____ _____

Problem 2

Pretend you have measured the following objects. Write the names of the objects in the proper column below.

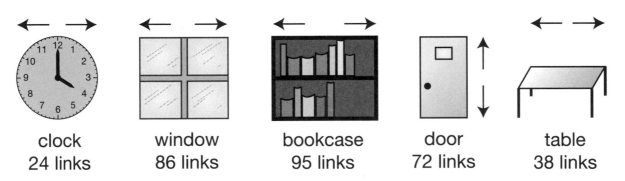

clock	window	bookcase	door	table
24 links	86 links	95 links	72 links	38 links

0–25 links	26–50 links	51–75 links	76–100 links

Problem 3

Write the number that each drawing of beans represents.

Problem 4

Draw a picture for this story. Solve the problem.

Alex had 15 marbles. Seven of them rolled under the stairs. How many marbles did he have then?

Problem 5

Make a triangle that is one toothpick long on each side. How many toothpicks would you need for 3 triangles? Show your work.

Problem 6

Look at the design:

Make the design longer; repeat the whole design 3 more times. How many more ▲ s do you need? Show your work.

Problem 7

You have 23 toothpicks. How many ⬜ s can you make? Show your work.

Problem 8

You need 2 inches of string to make one worm. You have 17 inches of string. How many worms can you make? Show your work.

Problem 9

Look at the calendar for the month of October.

Sunday	Monday	Tuesday	Wednesday	Thursday	Friday	Saturday
	1	2	3 Marta's birthday	4	5	6
7	8	9	10	11	12	13
14	15	16	17	18	19 School Play	20
21	22	23	24	25	26	27
28	29	30	31 Halloween			

A. What day of the week is the school play? _____

B. Ten days after Marta's birthday, she had a party. What day did she have the party? _____

Problem 10

$2 + 2 = \boxed{}$

$5 + \boxed{} = 8$

$\boxed{} + 9 = 11$

$6 + 3 = \boxed{}$

Problem 11

One inch of rain makes 10 inches of snow. Seven inches of rain fell. How many inches of snow would this have made? Show your work.

Problem 12

Juan uses $5\frac{1}{2}$ square inches of paper to cover a shape. Marta uses $7\frac{1}{2}$ square inches of paper to cover another shape. How many more square inches of paper does Marta use?

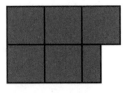

Problem 13

$4 + 4 = \boxed{}$

$8 + \boxed{} = 12$

$\boxed{} + 5 = 12$

$4 + 6 = \boxed{}$

Problem Solving

Problem 14

Draw the missing shape.

Draw the next shape in the pattern.

Problem 15

Georgina made a building. She used:
- 12 cubes on the first floor
- 8 cubes on the second floor
- 2 cubes on the third floor
- 1 cube on the top

How many cubes did she use altogether? Show your work.

Problem 16

You find a pile of 53 cubes. How many 8-cube buildings can you make? Show your work.

Problem 17

$\boxed{} + 6 = 14$ $\qquad$ $6 + 6 = \boxed{}$

$5 + \boxed{} = 14$ $\qquad$ $9 + 8 = \boxed{}$

Problem 18

Carlos begins with a 7-cube building. He wants to make a 26-cube building. How many cubes must he add? Show your work.

Problem 19

Twenty-seven children from the Springs School are going on a field trip. Each bus holds twelve children. How many buses will the Springs School need for the field trip? Show your work.

Problem 20

If you are in school 6 hours each day, how much time do you spend in school a week? Show your work.

Problem 21

10 + 9 = ☐

☐ + 10 = 16

3 + ☐ = 13

9 + 3 = ☐

Glossary

This glossary provides definitions or examples of key terms in the Grade 1 lessons as a resource for students and parents. See the Glossary in the *Teacher Implementation Guide* for more precise definitions.

A

Area (Unit 10)
The amount of space that a shape covers. Area is measured in square units.

B

C

Circumference (Unit 15)
The distance around a circle.

Counting All (Unit 1)
A strategy for counting and adding in which students start at one and count until the total is reached.

Counting On (Unit 1, Unit 4)
A strategy for counting or adding objects in which students start from a larger number and then count until the total is reached. For example, to count 6 + 3, begin with 6 and count three more, 7, 8, 9.

Cube (Unit 12, Unit 15)
A three-dimensional shape with six square faces that are all the same size.

Cubic Unit (Unit 12)
A unit for measuring volume—a cube that measures one unit along each edge. For example, cubic centimeters and cubic inches are standard units of measure.

cubic centimeter

Cylinder (Unit 15)
A three-dimensional shape. Examples:

Cylinders   Not a Cylinder

D

Data Table
A tool for recording and organizing information.

Name	Age

E

Edge (Unit 15)
A line segment where two faces of a three-dimensional figure meet.

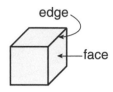

Estimate (Unit 12)
1. To find *about* how many (as a verb).
2. An approximate number (as a noun).

Even Number (Unit 4)
Numbers that are doubles. The numbers 0, 2, 4, 6, 8, 10, . . . etc. are even. The number 28 is even because it is 14 + 14.

F

Face (Unit 12)
A two-dimensional shape that is one side of a three-dimensional shape.

Fixed Variables (Unit 2, Unit 11)
Variables in an experiment that do not change.

G

H

Hexagon (Unit 2)
A six-sided polygon.

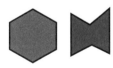 

Hexagons   Not Hexagons

I

J

K

L

Length
The distance along a line or curve from one point to another. Distance can be measured with a ruler or tape measure. Distance can also be measured in paces, handspans, and other nonstandard units.

Line
A set of points that form a straight path extending infinitely in two directions.

Line Symmetry (Unit 7, Unit 18)
A shape has line symmetry if it can be folded into two matching halves.

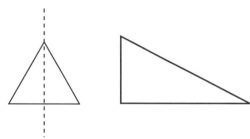

This shape has   This shape does not
line symmetry.   have line symmetry.

Line of Symmetry (Unit 7)
A line such that if a figure is folded along the line, then one half of the figure matches the other.

M

Making a Ten (Unit 13)
A strategy for adding and subtracting that takes advantage of students' knowledge of partitions of ten. For example, a student might find 8 + 4 by breaking the 4 into 2 + 2 and then using a knowledge of sums that add to ten.

$$8 + 4 =$$
$$8 + 2 + 2 =$$
$$10 + 2 = 12$$

Median (Unit 6, Unit 9)
The number "in the middle" of a set of data. Example 1: Jonah rolled a car down a ramp three times. The first time it rolled 30 cm. The second time it rolled 28 cm. The third time it rolled 33 cm. He put the numbers in order: 28 cm, 30 cm, 33 cm. The median is 30 cm because it is in the "middle" of his data. Example 2: The median of 28 cm, 30 cm, 32 cm, and 35 cm is 31 cm.

Mr. Origin (Unit 19)
A plastic figure used to help children learn about direction and distance.

N

Near Double (Unit 13)
A derived addition or subtraction fact found by using doubles. For example, $3 + 4 = 7$ follows from the fact that $3 + 3 = 6$.

Number Sentence (Unit 3)
A number sentence uses numbers and symbols instead of words to describe a problem. For example, a number sentence for the problem "Five birds landed on a branch. Then two more birds landed on the branch. How many birds are on the branch?" is $5 + 2 = 7$.

O

Odd Number (Unit 4)
A number that is not even. The odd numbers are 1, 3, 5, 7, 9, and so on.

Origin (Unit 6, Unit 19)
A reference point for a coordinate system. If the coordinate system is a line, we can determine the location of an object on the line by the number of units it is to the right or the left of the origin.

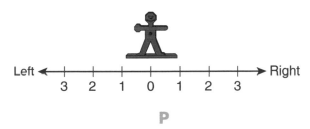

P

Pattern Unit (Unit 7)
The portion of a pattern that is repeated. For example, AAB is the pattern unit in the pattern AABAABAAB.

Perimeter (Unit 6)
The distance around a two-dimensional shape.

Polygon
A 2-dimensional shape. A closed, connected plane figure consisting of line segments, with exactly two segments meeting at each end point.

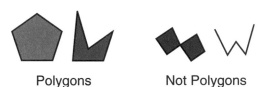

Polygons   Not Polygons

Prediction (Unit 5)
Using a sample to tell about what is likely to occur in a population.

Prism (Unit 15)
A three-dimensional shape. Examples:

Prisms   Not a Prism

Q

Quadrilateral
A polygon with four sides.

Quadrilaterals   Not a Quadrilateral

R

Rectangle (Unit 2)
A polygon with four sides and with four square corners.

Rectangles   Not a Rectangle

Rhombus (Unit 2)
A polygon with four sides of equal length.

Rhombuses   Not a Rhombus

S

Sample (Unit 5)
A smaller group taken out of a large collection.

Sphere (Unit 15)
A three-dimensional shape. A basketball is a common object shaped like a sphere.

Square (Unit 2)
A rectangle with four equal sides.

Squares   Not Squares

Symmetry (Unit 7, Unit 18)
See Line Symmetry

T

Three-dimensional Shape (Unit 15)
A figure in space that has length, width, and height.

TIMS Laboratory Method
A method that students use to organize experiments and investigations. It involves four components: draw, collect, graph, and explore. It is a way to help students learn about the scientific method. TIMS is an acronym for Teaching Integrated Mathematics and Science.

Trapezoid (Unit 2)
A shape with four sides with exactly one pair of parallel sides.

Trapezoids   Not Trapezoids

Trial (Unit 6)
One attempt in an experiment.

Triangle (Unit 2)
A polygon with three sides.

Triangles   Not a Triangle

U

Using Doubles (Unit 13)
A strategy for adding and subtracting that uses facts derived from known doubles. For example, students use $7 + 7 = 14$ to find that $7 + 8$ is one more, or 15.

Using Ten (Unit 13)
A strategy for adding and subtracting which uses reasoning from known facts. For example, students use $3 + 7 = 10$ to find that $4 + 7$ is one more, or 11.

V

Variable (Unit 2, Unit 11)
Something that changes or varies in an experiment.

Volume (Unit 9, Unit 12)
1. The amount of space an object takes up.
2. The amount of space inside a container (also called capacity).

W

X

Y

Z

Index

The index provides page references for the *Student Guide.* Definition or explanation of key terms can be found in the glossary. A good source for information on the location of topics in the curriculum is the *Scope and Sequence* in Section 5 of the *Teacher Implementation Guide.*